# REALLY WICKED

# IRISH
# JOKES

Other titles in this series:

**REALLY WICKED**

# IRISH JOKES

Compiled by David Brown

MICHAEL O'MARA BOOKS LTD

First published in Great Britain in 1998
by Michael O'Mara Books Limited
9 Lion Yard
Tremadoc Road
London SW4 7NQ

A CIP catalogue record for this book is available from the British Library

ISBN 1-85479-377-2

1 3 5 7 9 10 8 6 4 2

Cover design by Powerfresh

Designed and typeset by Design 23

Printed and bound in Great Britain by Cox & Wyman, Reading, Berks.

# IRISH

# FOLK

# LAW

Seamus was charged with deserting his wife.

"I award your wife £600 a month," said the judge.

"That's very generous of your honour," said Seamus. "I'll try and give her a few quid myself as well."

An Irishman was accused of robbing a girl, and was lined up in an identity parade. When the girl was brought into the police station to face the row of men, the Irishman pointed at her and said, "That's her."

Patrick was brought before the court, accused of selling a bottle of liquor without a licence.

"Look at this man," his lawyer said to the jury. "Do you really think that if he had a bottle of whiskey he would sell it?"

The jury took one look and found Patrick not guilty.

The Irishman was brought up before the judge.

"Why were you drunk?" the judge asked.

"I was on a train with bad companions. Four teetotallers," said the Irishman.

"They are the best company you can have," said the judge.

"I don't think so," said the Irishman, "I had a bottle of whiskey and had to drink it all by myself."

A drunk Irishman is standing, pissing into a fountain in the middle of town, so a policeman comes up to him and says, "Stop that and put it away."

The Irishman shoves his cock in his trousers and does up his zip. As the policeman turns to go, the Irishman starts laughing.

"OK. So what's so funny?" asks the copper.

"Fooled you," says the Irishman, "I may have put it away, but I didn't stop."

An Irishman who was working in an Arab country, where all alcohol was banned, was stopped at the Customs on his return from a visit home.

"What's in this bottle?" asked the customs officer, taking out a large bottle from the bottom of the Irishman's suitcase.

"That's a precious bottle of Holy Water from Lourdes that my dear mother gave me," replied the Irishman, who was a very quick thinker.

The customs officer unscrewed the top of the bottle and sniffed the liquid inside. Then he raised the bottle to his lips and took a little sip. "It smells and tastes very much like whiskey to me!" he said.

"Glory be to God!" said the Irishman. "'Tis another miracle!"

A man took his best suit to the dry-cleaners in Dublin. As he was collecting it he noticed there was a large soup stain on the front. When he pointed this out to the assistant she said to him, "You can't hold us responsible for that. It was there when you brought it in."

An Irishman stumbles out of a bar and is spied by a police constable. The constable approaches...

Constable: "Can I help ya lad?"

Man: "Yea, SSSSomebody ssstole my car!"

Constable: "Well, wheer was ya car last time ya saw it?"

Man: "It twas at the end of tiss key!" (he held up a key already in his hand).

Just then the constable notices the Irishman has his manhood out.

Constable: "Hey, ar ya aware ya expoosing yaself?"

Man: "Ohh God, they got me girl too!"

# BLESS ME FATHER

Two Irish nuns, Sister Mary Magdalen and Sister Mary Joseph, are driving back to the convent in their ancient Morris Minor, when suddenly a vampire bat lands on the bonnet of the car and sits there looking through the windscreen at them.

"Jesus, Mary and Joseph!" exclaims Sister Mary Magdalen. "Will ya look at that! We've got to do something about that evil creature! Show it yer cross, Sister!"

So Sister Mary Joseph winds down her window, leans out and shouts, "Get off my bloody bonnet!"

An Irishman was on board a plane waiting to take off to Dublin when a rumour began amongst all the passengers that the Pope was going to be on the same flight. The man was a staunch Catholic who revered the Pope and he was thrilled and amazed when the Holy Father was seated right next to him. He tried his best to keep cool and leave the Pope in peace, but he couldn't help noticing that the Pope was doing a crossword puzzle and seemed to be having some difficulty finishing it.

Suddenly the Pope turned to the Irishman and said, "Are you any good at crossword puzzles, my son? I'm having problems with this one."

The Irishman was overwhelmed by the fact that not only was he sitting next to the Holy Father, but also that he was being engaged in conversation by him. "Well I'm very fond of crosswords as it happens, perhaps I can help you," he answered.

"Oh good," said the Pope. "Can you think of a four letter word describing a woman that ends in 'UNT'?"

The Irishman was silent for a few moments

and then, looking relieved, said, "Yes, I have it: 'AUNT'."

"Thank you!" said the Pope. "Now, could you lend me a rubber?"

The priest and the minister found that they frequently travelled on the same bus together although, of course, they never exchanged a word. Eventually the minister decided that it would be a Christian act to break the silence and he said, "Good day, Father Curran. We seem to see each other rather often and I feel we really should be on speaking terms – after all, we're both in the same business, are we not?"

"Indeed we are," replied the priest. "But you're doing it your way and I'm doing it His!"

Early one morning in rural Ireland, a group of leprechauns knocked on the door of the convent and demanded to see the Mother Superior. When she came out they all stood there looking at her, in silence. So finally she said, "How can I help you?" at which one of the leprechauns stepped forward and asked,

"Mother Superior, are there any wee little leprechaun nuns here in this convent?"

Somewhat startled, the Mother Superior replied, "No, there aren't any wee little leprechaun nuns in this convent."

"Well then," continued the spokesman, "Are there any wee little leprechaun nuns in county Waterford?"

Confused, the Mother Superior said, "No, there are no wee little leprechaun nuns in county Waterford."

"Let me ask you one last question, then," said the leprechaun, "Do you know of any wee little leprechaun nuns in any convent, in any county in all of Ireland?"

Totally bewildered now, the Mother Superior answered, "I know of no wee little leprechaun nuns in any convent, in any county in the whole of Ireland."

The leprechauns all turned to one another, smiling and whispering, and gradually they got louder and louder until the Mother Superior finally heard what they were saying: "Paddy f**ked a penguin! Paddy f**ked a penguin!"

It was the stockbroker's first day in prison and on meeting his violent-looking Irish cell mate, he became even more nervous than ever.

"Don't worry, mister," said the prisoner, noticing how scared the stockbroker was looking, "I'm in for a white collar crime, too."

The stockbroker sat down on his bunk, weak with relief. "Thank goodness!" he said. "What was it you did?"

"Oh," the prisoner replied. "I murdered a priest."

Four Irish nuns go out for a weekend. On

Monday they come back and need to confess their sins. The first nun goes into the confessional and says, "Bless me, Father, for I have sinned. I touched a penis with this finger."

"You are forgiven," the priest replies. "Just swirl your finger in the holy water."

The second nun goes in. "Bless me, Father, for I have sinned. I fondled the private parts of a man with this hand."

And the priest says, "You are forgiven, Sister, just clean off your hand in the holy water."

The third nun was about to go into the confessional when the fourth nun says, "Sister Mary Patrick, please may I go in ahead of you? Otherwise I'll be drinking what you sit in."

An Irish Catholic went to confession. "Bless me, Father, for I have sinned. I had sex with a married woman."

"That is a mortal sin," the priest says. "You must tell me who she was."

"I can't do that, Father," the man replies. "It wouldn't be right."

"Was it Mary Stephens?"

"No."

"Was it Tricia O'Mara?"

The man shakes his head and says, "Please, Father, don't try to make me tell."

"If you won't tell me, then your penance will be fifty Hail Marys and fifty Our Fathers."

The priest sends the man away. Outside, he sees his friend, who's been waiting for him and who asks, "Did you tell him?"

"Yes."

"And what did you get?"

"Fifty Hail Marys, fifty Our Fathers and a couple of great tips."

An Irish priest meets a rabbi and they start to chat. "Tell me, Rabbi, have you ever eaten pork?" asks the priest.

"Well," replies the rabbi, "I once gave in to temptation and ate a ham sandwich. If we're exchanging special confidences, let me ask you something important: have you ever been with a woman?"

The priest looks sheepish but replies, "Yes, once, two years ago. I was at the end of my tether and tried the services of a prostitute in my parish."

"And what did you think of it?" enquires the rabbi.

"It beats the hell out of a ham sandwich," the priest replies.

In Ireland today, all the young girls stay out all night sowing their wild oats. And in the morning you can find them in church, praying for a crop failure.

Mary O'Donahue was eighty years old and a devout Catholic. Every day she walked the two miles to attend Mass at the local church, and every Friday she went to confession. She had followed this routine all her life. One Friday she went in to the confessional and said," Bless me, Father, for I have sinned. I have committed adultery with a seventeen-year-old gardener's boy."

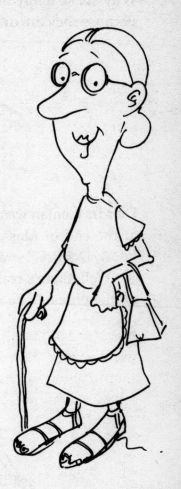

The priest was absolutely horrified. "Good heavens, Mary O'Donahue, and when was that?"

"Oh, a good fifty years ago, Father, but I felt like recalling some pleasant experiences this week."

Why are so many Irish priests alcoholics?
Because they are drawn to the pure in spirit.

Deirdre Conlan was talking to the village priest at the end of Mass, and the priest said, "You know, Deirdre, I pray for you every night."

"Well, there's really no need to, Father, I am on the phone," she replied.

# DOCTOR, DOCTOR

The Belfast doctor's waiting room was very full. All the chairs were taken and some patients were having to stand. At first there was some conversation in the room, but as the time passed the room became even more crowded and the patients sat and waited in silence. At last an old man struggled wearily to his feet and as he turned to leave he said, "Well now, I think I'll just go home to my bed and die a natural death."

An Irish country woman went to her doctor and asked to be put on birth control pills. The doctor told her that it would be illegal in Ireland, but she said, with ten kids in ten years and still only thirty years old herself, what could she do?

The doctor suggested that she go back to the farm and cut the top off a two gallon paraffin tin. If she slept with both feet in the tin every night, she would not become pregnant.

Six months later she was back to see him again, very obviously pregnant. "I thought I told you..."

"I know you did, Doctor," the woman interrupted. "But you see he buys his paraffin in one gallon tins, so I put one on each foot."

Did you hear about the Irishman who lost his licence to practise medicine?

He was caught having sex with some of his patients. It's such a shame – he was by far the best vet in the county.

A woman goes to an Irish doctor and says, "Doctor, my husband limps because his left leg is an inch shorter than his right leg. What would you do in his case?"

"Probably limp, too," says the doctor.

The psychiatrist was advising the depressed Irishman.

"Find yourself a girl who likes to do the things you do," he said.

"But, Doctor," the Irishman protested. "What would I be wanting with a girl who likes to whistle at other girls?"

# THE SPORTING IRISH

Did you hear about the Irish sky diver?

He was killed when his snorkel and flippers failed to open.

Brendan McCann walked into his local fishmonger's early one morning and asked to buy half a dozen trout. "Certainly, Brendan." the fishmonger replied, and started to wrap them.

"No, no!" Brendan exclaimed. "Please don't wrap them up. Can you just throw them to me gently, one by one?"

"Well, I can, but why on earth would you want me to do that?" asked the fishmonger.
"You see," Brendan replied, "I've been out fishing the stream all night long without a sniff of a bite and if you throw those trout to me and I catch them, I can honestly tell Molly when I get home that I caught six trout."

The great Irish game hunter was stalking in the jungles of Africa, when he stumbled across a beautiful woman, lying naked in a clearing.

"Begorrah!" he said, "Are you game?"

She gave a seductive smile and said, "Why, yes, I am!"

So he shot her.

Two Irishmen bought themselves a horse each and decided to keep them in the same field.

"How shall we tell which horse is which?" Paddy asked Sean.

"I'll tie a green ribbon to my horse's tail," replied Sean.

Unfortunately, the ribbon on Sean's horse fell off one day in his absence, so the two of them were again faced with the problem of deciding which horse was which.

"I know!" said Paddy. "You have the brown horse and I'll have the white one."

A young Irishman walks into a chemist's shop and asks for a box of tampons. The sales assistant is surprised and says, "Young man, what do you want with tampons?"

"Well," says the young man, "my sister says that if you use them, you can run, go horseback riding, and take part in all kinds of dangerous sports."

Did you hear about the Irish skier with frost-bite on his bottom?

He couldn't figure out how to get his trousers over his skis.

A German bobsleigh team was competing in the Winter Olympics. Suddenly there was a terrible crash. The German team met the Irish team coming up.

# WORK,

# WORK,

# WORK.

The foreman on a building site was really annoyed to see that a new wall had been laid crooked. He called his bricklayer over and said, "Pat, this is a terrible piece of work you've done! Look here where it's all crooked and twisted!"

Pat replied, "It's right you are. Bad luck to the fella Lynch, he never sold a straight piece of string in his life."

Mrs Smith's doorbell stopped working, so she rang and made an appointment for an electrician to come over and repair it that afternoon. She waited in until the evening but he never showed up. So the next morning she was surprised to see a man in overalls coming up her garden path. She opened the door to him and he said, "Hello there, Mrs. Smith, I'm Paddy, the electrician."

"Why didn't you come yesterday like you were supposed to? I waited in for hours."

"Oh, I did come yesterday," said Paddy. "But after I'd rung the bell three times and got no reply, I thought you must be out."

"Jesus," Mike said to Seamus at the construction site, "You've been working really hard today!"

Seamus winked and replied, "I'm just foolin' the boss. I've been carryin' the same load of bricks up and down the stairs all day long!"

Two Irishmen drove up to the wood yard, but only one of them got out. He was an apprentice carpenter and was making his first buy on his own. He walked up to the man at the counter and announced, "I'd like some four by fours."

The man eyed him suspiciously and asked, "You mean two by fours, don't you?"

The young man shook his head. "I'm sure the boss said four by fours," he said.

"Is that him sitting in the car?" The young man nodded. "Do me a favour, then, and just go and ask him exactly how long you want them."

Shrugging, the young man went back to the car. When he returned he said, "We're building a house, the boss says, and we want them forever."

Overheard in an Irish pub:

"Can you lend me ten pounds till pay day?"

"When's pay day?"

"How should I know.  You're the one who's working."

Why don't the Irish look out of the window in the morning at work?

Because then they'd have nothing to do in the afternoon.

An Irish telephone engineer was trying to measure a telephone pole but he couldn't figure out how to climb up it. He radioed his office and his supervisor suggested that he lay the pole down on the ground to measure it. The Irishman didn't much like the idea.

"That won't work," he said. "I need to measure how high it is, not how long."

How can you keep an Irishman busy?
    Give him two shovels and tell him to take his pick.

How many Irish blokes does it take to change a light bulb?
    None, that's women's work.

# WEDDED BLISS

"How's your wife getting on, Seamus?"

"Well, sometimes she's better and sometimes she's worse. But from her goin's on when she's better, I often think that she's better when she's worse."

"I presume, Mrs. Murphy, that you carry some sort of memento in that locket of yours?" enquired her neighbour one day.

"Indeed I do, Mrs. Nolan, it's a lock of my Dan's hair"

"But your husband is still alive, Mrs. Murphy."

"Indeed he is, Mrs. Nolan, but his hair's been gone a long time."

What do you call an Irish couple who use the rhythm method of birth control?

Parents.

Why did the Irish newlyweds stay up all night?

They were waiting for their sexual relations to arrive.

This old Irish couple had been married for thirty years and they decided to revisit the same little hotel that they'd spent their honeymoon in, all those years before. As they were driving through the countryside, the old man said, "Well, my lovely, I want to touch you the same way I did thirty years ago."

"You may, you old devil," his wife replied, and he put his hand on her knee. A few miles later he touched her on the arm and said, "Maureen, look where we are. Let's do the same thing we did thirty years ago." He stopped the car and they both got out and made passionate love, standing up against a wire fence.

"Oh, my love," said the husband, after they had both finished and had resumed their journey. "Thirty years ago you didn't move against me like you moved just now!"

"Thirty years ago," said his wife, "That fence wasn't electrified."

An Irishwoman went to the Citizen's Advice Bureau to ask about obtaining a divorce.

"Does your husband beat you?"

"No, he's a kind, gentle man."

"Does he drink and gamble?"

"No, he gives all his wages to me."

"Then, of course, unfaithfulness must be the trouble."

"Yes, I suppose it must be. One of the children isn't his."

An Irish couple in their thirties were discussing important matters at home after supper.

"I don't think we should have any more kids," said the wife.

"But why not, dear?" said her husband. "I thought you always wanted four."

"Not any more," she replied. "I've just heard on the radio that every fourth child born in the world today is Chinese."

An Irish couple, who had been saving up for five years, were taking a cruise for their honeymoon. Their very first evening on board, they received a note in their cabin asking them to sit at the Captain's table for dinner that evening.

"I don't believe it!" complained the bridegroom to his new wife. "We've waited five long years and spent all that money that we saved paying for this cruise, and we still have to eat with the crew!"

Christy and Maureen decided to adopt a Romanian baby, and sent their application off to the agency with very high hopes. Sure enough, a letter came the following week confirming that a six month-old baby would be delivered to them within a fortnight. Christy and Maureen were so excited that they rushed out to sign up for Romanian language classes, so that they would be able to understand their baby when he was old enough to talk.

Mr. and Mrs. O'Reilly had been trying for a son for many, many years and, after eleven healthy daughters they were finally rewarded with a son.

"Who does he look like?" asked a friend visiting the maternity ward to congratulate the proud mother.

"Oh, we don't know," replied Mrs. O'Reilly. "We haven't looked at his face yet."

Liam snored loudly – so loudly that his wife Moira used to say, "I swear, Liam, one of these days you'll snore your guts up!" This went on for years, until one day Moira couldn't take it any more. That afternoon she went to the butcher and bought a sheep's heart, some chicken livers and some pig's kidneys. That night, while he was snoring away, she arranged them all round Liam's head, on the pillows.

The next morning Liam stumbled downstairs to breakfast, white faced. "What's the matter, Liam, you look terrible?"

"You'll not believe this, Moira. I always thought you were just winding me up, but you were right! When I woke up this morning I'd snored my guts up!"

"Never!" said Moira. "We'd better get you to the hospital."

"Oh, no, it's O.K. now." he said. "By the grace of God, and with the aid of a toothbrush, I managed to get them all back down."

As a woman rushed with a kettle to pour water over her burning curtains, her husband shouted at her: "Don't be a fool, Mary. To be sure that water's no good – it's boiling!"

A highly excited Irishman rang up for an ambulance. "Quickly, come quickly," he shouted, "my wife's about to have a baby."

"Is this her first baby?" asked the operator.

"No, you idiot," came the reply, "it's her husband."

# NATURAL GENIUS

What's three miles long, green, and has an IQ of 10?

The Saint Patrick's Day parade.

The cashier at this car wash in Kilburn says to this man, "Hello there! Seeing an Irishman like you here this morning has really cheered me up."

"How in the name of God did you know I was Irish?" asks the man, astonished.

"Well, we don't get many people riding motorbikes in here."

The tough guy sauntered into the dimly lit bar. "Is there anybody here called Flaherty?" he snarled. No-one answered. Again he snarled, "Is there anybody here called Flaherty?"

There were a few moments silence and then a little fellow stepped forward. "I'm Flaherty," he said.

The tough guy picked him up and threw him across the bar. Then he punched him in the jaw, kicked him, clubbed him, slapped him around a bit and walked out. About ten minutes later the little fellow came to. "Boy, did I fool him," he said. "I ain't Flaherty."

One Irish shopkeeper to another:

"How's business, Kevin?"

"Terrible, Tom, terrible. The month before last I lost £1000. Last month I lost £2000."

"So why don't you shut up shop, then?"

"But how would I make a living?"

At the start of the new school year, the teacher was getting to know all the pupils and said to one boy, "Are you Irish?"

"Yes, I am." he replied.

"What's your name?" the teacher enquired.

"Pat." he answered.

"You can't be true Irish," said the teacher. "If you were true Irish you'd say, 'Patrick'." And, turning to the boy's friend, the teacher said, "So, what's your name, then?"

"Mickrick," came the reply.

Why wasn't the Irishman worried when his car was stolen?

He got the licence plate number.

An Irish family were arguing vehemently over their eldest daughter's choice of fiancé.

"But, Mother!" she cried, "He says he'll put the whole earth at my feet!"

"You've already got the whole earth at your feet." replied her mother. "What you'll be needing is a roof over your head!"

Dominic O'Reilly went into a bank to withdraw a large sum of money.

"Can you identify yourself?" asked the teller.

Dominic pulled a mirror out of his pocket, peered into it and said, "Sure I can. That's me all right."

An Irishman was telling his friend that he thought he'd seen a ghost one night, so he picked up his shotgun and shot it. When he got up in the morning he found it was only his shirt. "What did you do then?" asked his friend.

"I knelt down and thanked God I wasn't in it".

What's the difference between an Irishman and a computer?

You only have to punch information into a computer once.

Did you hear the one about the Irishman who wanted to be buried at sea?

Six of his mates were drowned trying to dig a hole.

It was Connor and Brendan's first longhaul flight and they were heading off to Bali. They were due to land in about an hour when the pilot made an announcement. "Good afternoon, ladies and gentlemen. As you probably know, we are roughly an hour from Bali but unfortunately we've lost one of our four engines. We will therefore be landing half an hour later than scheduled but there is no need for alarm, so just sit back and enjoy the flight."

Fifteen minutes later he made another announcement. "Ladies and gentlemen, this is the Captain speaking. We have lost a second engine, but I repeat: there is absolutely no cause for alarm. We are, however, an hour behind schedule."

Ten more minutes passed before the Captain, this time sounding distinctly nervous, announced, "Ladies and gentlemen, we have now lost a third engine and we will now be arriving in Bali two hours behind schedule. I repeat, there is no cause for alarm. Please enjoy your flight but remain in your seats with your seat belts fastened."

"Mother of God!" said Connor, who had been paying close attention to the proceedings, "I hope we don't lose the last damn engine or we'll be up here all day!"

Travelling through Bali, Connor and Brendan decided to split up and do a bit of exploring on their own. When they met up again later in the evening, Connor was driving a gleaming white Porsche. "Good God!" said Brendan, "Where'd you get that from?"

"Well," said Connor, "I was walking through the town, having a bit of a look round, when suddenly this car drew up beside me, and this beautiful blonde woman offered to show me the countryside. We drove for a while and then she pulled off the road, in the middle of nowhere, took a picnic basket out of the back, and we had a great meal. Then she took off all her clothes, lay back on the blanket and told me to take whatever I wanted. So I took the car."

"Good thinking, Connor!" said Brendan. "You'd look pretty damn silly in her clothes."

How can you spot an Irish aeroplane?
   It's got an outside loo.

Did you hear about the two gay Irishmen?
   Their names were Patrick Fitzjohn and John
Fitzpatrick

What do you call an Irishman with half a brain?
   Gifted.

A travelling saleswoman from Belfast was driving through a remote, rural area in southern Ireland when her car broke down. She took to the road and eventually came across a small farmhouse. On the porch sat two brothers in rocking chairs.

"How far is it to the nearest petrol station?" she asked.

"About twenty miles, I reckon," said one of the brothers.

"Well, how far is it to the nearest hotel?"

"About thirty miles," said the other brother.

"Could you drive me there?"

"No, we don't have a car."

Despairing, the woman said, "Well, could I possibly stay here tonight? I suppose I'll have to try to hitch a ride tomorrow."

"Well now, sure you can – but you'll have to share our room."

The woman had no other choice but to agree. So before she got into the bed that night, she handed each man a condom and said, "Please wear these so I won't get pregnant."

The next morning, she left. Three months later the two brothers were sitting outside on the porch when one said to the other, "Paddy, do you really care if that Belfast woman gets pregnant?"

"Nope."

"Then how about we take these damn things off then?"

A tourist went in to a pub in Dublin, and sitting at the bar was an Irishman with the biggest dog he had ever set eyes on.

"Does your dog bite?" the tourist asked.

"No," the Irishman replied, "My dog is as gentle as a lamb."

So the tourist, reassured, went over and patted the dog and the dog nearly bit his hand off.

"I thought you just told me your dog didn't bite!" he shouted at the Irishman.

"He doesn't," came the reply. "But this isn't my dog."

Why did the Irish stop making ice?

Because the old lady who knew the recipe died.

What do you call an Irishman standing in the middle of a paddock?

A thicket.

Declan was woken by the phone ringing in the middle of the night, so he got out of bed to answer it.

"Hello?" said the caller. "Is that seven-six-double-three-double-three?"

"No," said Declan, "this is seven-six-three-three-three-three."

"Oh. Sorry to have disturbed you," said the caller.

"That's OK," said Declan. "I had to get up anyway. The phone was ringing."

Passing an office building late one night, an Irishman saw a sign that said, "Press bell for night watchman."

He pressed the bell, and after several minutes he heard the watchman clumping down the stairs. The uniformed man proceeded to unlock first one gate, then another, shut down the alarm system and finally made his way through the revolving door.

"Well," he said grumpily to the Irishman, "what do you want at this hour?"

"I just wanted to know why you can't ring it yourself."

They were sitting by the fire with steaming cups of coffee, relaxing after a hard day's work. Desmond's dog was licking his private parts, and Noel watched him enviously. "Y'know," he said, "I've always wanted to be able to do that."

"Well, it wouldn't bother me," said the ever-generous Desmond, "but I'd pat him a bit, first. He can be a bit vicious at times."

After ordering the extra large pizza at the local pizzeria, the Irishman added, "And make sure you only cut it in three pieces. I could never eat six."

An Irishman picks up a woman in a pub and asks her to come back to his place. She says, "I'd love to, but I have my menstrual cycle."

"Oh, that's OK," the man replies, "we can put it in the boot."

The hotel clerk told the Irishman that there were no more rooms with a bath, and asked whether he would mind sharing a bath with another of the male guests.

"No," replied the Irishman, "as long as he stays at his end of the bath."

An Irishman goes to the travel agency and says, "I'd like a round-trip ticket, please."

"Where to?" the assistant asks.

"Why, back here, of course."

Did you hear about the Irishman who bought an A.M. radio?

It took him months before he realized he could play it at night too.

"I wish I had a watch that tells the time," said Seamus.

"Doesn't your watch tell the time?" his friend inquired.

"No," Seamus said dejectedly, "I have to look at it."

Brendan went to a smart London restaurant with his wife and ordered an expensive bottle of wine.

"Certainly, Sir," said the wine waiter, "which year?"

"I'll have it right away," said Brendan, "if you don't mind."

Paddy was filling in the application form to join a new club.

At the bottom of the form, where it said 'Sign here,' he wrote, 'Capricorn.'

Did you hear about the Irishman who heard the country was at war?

He moved to the city.

What's the difference between a cheese sandwich and an Irishman?

A cheese sandwich is only half an inch thick.

What's the difference between a hundred cheese sandwiches and an Irishman?

Nothing.

How many Irishman does it take to change a light bulb?

Two. One to hold the bulb, and one to drink until the room starts spinning.

The Aer Lingus plane was in serious trouble over the sea.

"May day, May day, May day," radioed the Captain.

"We've got you on the screen," the air controller answered, "What's the problem? Can you give us your exact height and position?"

"Well now," replied the Captain, "I'm five foot ten and a half and I'm sitting at the front of the plane."

# THE
# DEMON
# DRINK

Two old Irish drunks were drinking in the pub together, when the first one says: "You know, Mick, when I was 30 and got a hard-on, I couldn't bend it with both hands. When I was 40, I could bend it about 10 degrees if I tried really hard. By the time I was 50, I could bend it about 20 degrees, no problem. I'm 60 next week and now I can almost bend it in half with just one hand."

"So," says the second drunk, "What's your point?"

"The point is, I'm just wondering how much stronger I'm going to get."

Old Dolan always was nosy. When the new neighbours moved in next door, he stood by the window and studied every piece of furniture that went into the place. There wasn't much, only a load of beer barrels.

"Begorrah, Mabel," he called out. "They're having the place nicely furnished next door."

Tim was on holiday in Ireland, staying at a small country pub. One evening he was amazed to overhear the following conversation:

"That's a beautiful hat you've got there," said an old boy to a young fellow who was standing next to him at the bar. "Where did you buy it?"

"At O'Grady's," replied the young man.

"Why, I go there myself," commented the old boy. "You must be a local chap then?"

"Aye, I am – from Murphy Street."

"Well, by all the saints, what a coincidence!" exclaimed the old boy. "That's where I'm from too!"

"That's amazing," said Tim to the barman, "That those two people live in the same street and have only just met."

"Don't you believe it!" said the barman. "They're actually father and son but they're always too drunk to recognize each other!"

A drunk staggered into Limerick churchyard and fell asleep amongst the tombstones. Early the next morning he was woken by the sound of a local factory hooter and, seeing where he was, concluded, not unnaturally, that he had heard Gabriel's trumpet. "Boy, oh boy," he said to himself, "Not a soul risen but me! This speaks badly for Limerick."

Did you hear about the queer Irishman?
    He preferred women to whiskey.

There was an old club man in St. Stephen's Green who always drank his whiskey with his eyes closed. When he was asked to explain his strange habit, he said, "It's like this: whenever I see a glass of whiskey my mouth waters, and I don't care to dilute it."

Paddy was taking a short-cut home through the fields one night after leaving the pub, when he thought he heard a little voice saying, "Help, please help me!" Peering about, he could see no-one but starting off on his way, he heard the voice again. This time he had a good search around and finally found a little leprechaun with his foot caught in a trap. Paddy carefully freed the leprechaun who said, "I'm in your debt, kind Sir, and I'd like to repay your kindness by offering you three wishes."

"Why, thank you," said Paddy, "I wish I had a bottle of whiskey in me hand right now!"

No sooner had he spoken than a bottle of whiskey appeared in his hand, and he unscrewed the cap and took a swig.

"You've two more wishes," said the leprechaun, "and I don't want to rush you but I must be getting along soon."

"OK, then," said Paddy, "I wish this bottle would never get empty!"

"Done!" said the leprechaun, and sure enough, every time Paddy had another swig, the bottle filled itself up again.

"And for your third wish?" enquired the leprechaun.

"Begorrah," slurred Paddy, waving the magic bottle around, "I think I'll have another one of these."

An Irishman is sitting at a bar and is already three sheets to the wind. He asks the barman for another Guinness and throws it down. He has six more beers until he can hardly speak. He says to the barman, "Gghive me shone shmore." The barman refuses to serve him.

The Irishman gets livid and says to the man, "You llllisthen chere buddy. I'm payin ya goooood smoneys to have a Guinessh, you gives me one rightsh f**king shnow!"

The barman doesn't want any trouble so he gives him another Guinness. The drunk downs it and demands another. Again wanting no trouble, the barman decides to make a deal with him.

So he says to the Irishman, "Listen here lad, I'll only give you another one on three conditions – you must do three things for me."

The drunk says, "Okay, just give me a f**king beer."

The barman begins his commands, "First, see that bouncer over there? He's new and I need you to pick a fight with him and test him out." (The bouncer is absolutely huge and the barman knows that the drunk stands no chance.)

The drunk stands up from the bar, walks up to the bouncer, looks up and lays him out with one punch, returns to the bar and demands a beer.

The barman says, "Wait, there are two more things you must do next – there's a guard dog in the back all chained up who's got a tooth ache. He's a vicious animal and doesn't let anyone near him. You must go and pull his bad tooth. Then when you're done with that, I've got a sister upstairs who's ugly as sin and will never get fucked as long as she lives. She's feeling pretty bad about herself. Go upstairs and give her a good time. When you're done with them, come back here and I'll treat you for the rest of the day to all the brew you want."

The drunk gets up, goes in the backroom and all you could hear was the dog squealing.

The drunk comes back to the bar all sweaty and says, "Okay, so whersh your shishter with the bad tooth?"

Brenda O'Malley is home as usual, making dinner, when Tim Finnegan arrives at her door.

"Brenda, may I come in?" he asks. "I've somethin' to tell ya."

"Of course you can come in, you're always welcome, Tim. But where's me husband, Seamus?"

"That's what I'm here to be tellin' ya, Brenda. There was an accident down at the brewery..."

"Oh, God no!" cries Brenda. "Please don't tell me..."

"I must, Brenda. Seamus is dead and gone. I'm sorry."

Brenda reached a hand out to her side, found the arm of the rocking chair by the fireplace, pulled the chair to her and collapsed into it. She wept for many minutes. Finally she looked up at Tim: "Tell me, how did it happen, Tim?"

"T'was terrible, Brenda. He fell into a vat of Guinness Stout and drowned."

"Oh dear Jesus! But you must tell me true, Tim. Did he at least go quickly?"

"Well, no Brenda. I'm sorry to say, it wasn't quick at all."

"Oh, dear God, me poor Seamus!"

"Fact is, he got out three times to piss."

A man stumbles up to the only other patron in a bar and asks if he could buy him a drink. "Why, of course," comes the reply.

The first man then asks: "Where are you from?"

"I'm from Ireland," replies the second man.

The first man responds, "You don't say, I'm from Ireland too! Let's have another round to Ireland."

"Of course," replies the second man.

Curious, the first man then asks: "Where in Ireland are you from?"

"Dublin," comes the reply.

"I can't believe it," says the first man. "I'm from Dublin too! Let's have another drink to Dublin."

"Of course," replies the second man.

Curiosity again strikes and the first man asks, "What school did you go to?"

"Saint Mary's," replies the second man, "I graduated in '62."

"This is unbelievable!", the first man says. "I went to Saint Mary's and I graduated in '62, too!"

About that time, in comes one of the regulars and sits down at the bar. "What's been going on?" he asks the barman.

"Nothing much," replies the barman. "The O'Mally twins are drunk again."

An Irishman has been at a pub all night, drinking. The barman finally says that the bar is closed. So he stands up to leave and falls flat on his face.

He decides that he'll crawl outside and get some fresh air and maybe that will sober him up. Once outside he stands up and falls flat on his face. So he crawls home and at the door stands up and falls flat on his face. He crawls through the door and up the stairs.

When he reaches his bed he tries one more time to stand up. This time he falls right into bed and is immediately asleep. He wakes up the next morning with his wife standing over him, shouting at him.

"So, you've been out drinking again!"

"How did you know?" he asks.

"The pub called, you left your wheelchair there again."

An old Irishman moved from his village to another closer to the hospital as he was beginning to age a bit.

He went into the local pub and ordered three pints of Guinness Stout. When he drank, he drank one sip from the first, the second, and then the third. After drinking like this for a while, he finally finished all three glasses. He took them up to the bartender for a refill.

The bartender said, "Ya know me friend, if ya were to drink this beer one glass at a time it would be a might fresher and bit more enjoyable."

The man replied, "Ay, a reckon so, but me two brothers and I agreed to drink our beer this way ever since they emigrated to the United States. It's our way of remembrin' one another."

The bartender replied, "Aw now, that makes sense."

The man became a regular and one day came in and ordered only two beers. He drank those in his normal fashion, sipping from each glass one at a time. The other locals and the bartender were quiet and hushed.

When the man came up for a refill the bartender said, "Me friend I am sorry about ya los'n ya brother."

The man replied, "Aw naw, it's noth'n like that, it's just that I stopped drink'n."

McAteer arrived at Heathrow Airport and wandered about the terminal with tears streaming down his cheeks. An airline employee asked him if he was already homesick.

"No," replied McAteer, "I've lost all me luggage!"

"How did that happen?" the man asked.

"The cork fell out," said the Irishman.

# FOREIGN
# EXCHANGE

It was the annual meeting of the International Federation of Space Scientists in 2050. "We are preparing to send a rocket to Pluto", announced the American, proudly. "It will carry six men and will stay on Pluto for an entire month carrying out a series of tests and experiments before returning to Earth."

"That's nothing compared to our programme!" jeered the Russian. "We're just about to launch our spaceship carrying two hundred men and women who are going to start the first colony on Uranus!"

"Well my country can beat you both," said the Irish scientist. "We're going to send a rocket

straight to the Sun!"

"Don't be ridiculous!" scoffed the American and the Russian. "The rocket will melt long before it gets there."

"Oh no it won't!" replied the Irishman. "We're sending it up at night."

An Irishman, a Scotsman and an Englishman were fishing from a cliff, when one of them hauled up an old bottle on the end of his line. When he pulled it off the line, he gave it a quick wipe and suddenly a genie appeared in a swirling cloud of blue smoke.

"Thank you for releasing me from this ancient curse," he boomed. "I will grant you one wish. Leap from the top of this cliff, call out the name of whatever you desire and you will land safely in a boat at the bottom, in a bountiful pile of that which you named." And with that, he vanished in another puff of blue smoke.

The Englishman thought for a while and then leapt off the cliff shouting,"Gold!" To his relief, he landed safely in a dinghy which was brimming with gold sovereigns.

"Diamonds!" shouted the Scotsman, flinging himself off the cliff. He too landed safely, in a glittering boat loaded with diamonds. And the Irishman? Well, he just didn't think. The excitement was just too much for him: as he jumped off the cliff he yelled, "Whee!"

A man walked out of his house in Belfast and another man came up to him and put a gun to his head saying, "Are you a Catholic or a Protestant?"

The first man was afraid of getting shot, so he said, "As a matter of fact, I'm neither, I'm Jewish."

"Well," the gunman responded, "I must be the luckiest Arab in Belfast tonight!"

There was a German, an Italian and an Irishman on top of a a big construction platform. The German opened his lunch box, saw it contained sauerkraut and said, "If I haff this stuff vun more time, I vill jump off zis beam!"

The Italian then looked in his box, saw pasta and said, "If I 'av dissa pasta one more time, I jump offa dis beam!"

Then the Irishman looked in his box and saw a cheese and tomato sandwich. "If I have this sandwich one more time," he says, "I swear to Almighty God I'll jump off this beam!"

The next day the German opened his box, saw sauerkraut and immediately jumped off the beam. Then the Italian looked in his box,

saw pasta and jumped off the beam, too. The Irishman looked in his box, saw a cheese and tomato sandwich, and jumped off the beam as well.

The three workers' wives were summoned to the scene and the boss told them what had happened. He also said he had overheard their conversation the previous day, threatening to jump if they had to keep eating the same lunch. All three women were in tears but then the German wife spoke up, "Dat's very vierd, he neffer said anyzing to me. If he had I would neffer have packed it!" Then the Italian wife said exactly the same thing. But the Irish wife, who was crying her heart out by now, sobbed: "I just don't understand it, because my Daniel always packs his own lunch!"

An Englishman, a Scotsman and an Irishman were stranded on a desert island in the Indian Ocean. One day they found a magic bottle and when they rubbed it, a genie appeared and granted them each one wish.

"I'd like to be back in London," said the Englishman and he was whisked away.

"I'd like to be back in Glasgow," said the Scot and he too was whisked away.

"I'm very lonely here all on my own," said the Irishman, "I wish my friends were back again."

A Scotsman, an Englishman and an Irishman were all due to face a firing squad in the morning, so they spent most of the night working out their plan of escape. The Scotsman came up with the best idea: "We'll each think of a means to distract them and when they are turning their backs, the one who creates the distraction can run away into the jungle. I'll go first and show you."

The others agreed, and so in the morning they were lined up in front of the soldiers who were just about to shoot them, when suddenly the Scotsman shouted "Hurricane!" The whole squad turned to look and the Scotsman ran off into the jungle.

Next it was the Englishman's turn, and as the squad took aim at him, he shouted, "Flash flood!" Again the firing squad turned to look and the Englishman ran off into the jungle.

Then it was the Irishman's turn, and as the guns were aimed at him, he quickly yelled out, "Fire!"

An Englishman, a Scotsman and an Irishman were driving through the Sahara desert when their four-wheel drive broke down and they decided to walk until they found an oasis.

The Englishman said, "I'll take the water so we'll have something to drink."

An Englishman, a Scotsman and an Irishman were sentenced to death by guillotine while travelling through a far distant country.

The Englishman placed his head on the block and the guillotine came crashing down – and stopped before it reached his neck.

"Praise be to God!" roared the watching crowd. "The prisoner is blessed, he can go free!"

The Scotsman then knelt down and placed his head on the block. Once again the guillotine came crashing down...and stopped before it reached his neck.

"God is great!" shouted the crowd. "The prisoner is blessed and he can go free!"

Then it was the turn of the Irishman. As he knelt to place his head on the block, he looked up and noticed that the blade was catching on a rusty nail. "There you are then," he said, pointing, "the problem's right here."

An Englishman, an Irishman and a Scotsman were sitting in a bar, drinking and discussing how stupid their wives were.

The Englishman says, "I tell you, my wife is so stupid. Last week she went to the supermarket and bought £200 worth of meat because it was on sale, and we don't even have a fridge to keep it in."

The Scotsman agrees that she sounds pretty thick, but says his wife is thicker. "Just last week, she went out and spent £12,000 on a new car," he laments, "and she doesn't even know how to drive!" The Irishman nods sagely, and agrees that these two woman both sound pretty dim.

However, he still thinks his wife is sillier. "Ah, it kills me every time oi tink of it," he chuckles. "Moy woife just left to go on a holiday in Greece. Oy watched her packing her bag, and she must have put about 100 condoms in there. And she doesn't even have a penis!"

Several years ago, Great Britain funded a study to determine why the head on a man's penis is larger than the shaft. The study took two years and cost over £$^1$/$_2$ million.

The study concluded that the reason the head of a man's penis is larger than the shaft was to provide the man with more pleasure during sex.

After the results were published, France decided to conduct their own study on the same subject. They were convinced that the results of the British study were incorrect.

After three years of research at a cost of in excess of £1 million, the French researchers concluded that the head of a man's penis is larger than the shaft to provide the woman with more pleasure during sex.

When the results of the French study were released, Ireland decided to conduct their own study. The Irish didn't really trust British or French studies.

So, after nearly three weeks of intensive research and a cost of about £50, the Irish study was complete. It concluded that the reason the head on a man's penis is larger than the shaft is to prevent your hand from flying off and hitting you in the forehead.